MESOPOTAMIA

for Elsa

❖

With thanks to Megan Cifarelli,
Norbert Schimmel Fellow in the Art of the Mediterranean
at The Metropolitan Museum of Art, New York City,
for her assistance in reading the manuscript.

CULTURES
OF THE PAST

MESOPOTAMIA

PAMELA F. SERVICE

BENCHMARK BOOKS

MARSHALL CAVENDISH
NEW YORK

Benchmark Books
Marshall Cavendish Corporation
99 White Plains Road
Tarrytown, New York 10591-9001

© Marshall Cavendish Corporation 1999

Library of Congress Cataloging-in-Publication Data

Service, Pamela F.
   Ancient Mesopotamia / Pamela F. Service.
     p.   cm.— (Cultures of the past)
   Includes bibliographical references and index.
   Summary: Discusses the history, social order, customs, religion, and accomplishments of the area known as the "cradle of civilization."
   ISBN 0-7614-0301-9
   1. Iraq—Civilization—To 634—Juvenile literature. [1. Iraq—Civilization—To 634.] I. Title. II. Series.
DS69.5.S47   1999
935—dc21   96-54611

Printed in China
6

Book design by Carol Matsuyama
Photo research by Debbie Needleman

Front cover: Sumerian temple statue, from c. 2500 B.C.E.
Back cover: The ruins of ancient Uruk, an important Sumerian city.

Photo Credits

Front cover: courtesy of Louvre, Paris/Bridgeman Art Library International, Ltd., London/New York; back cover: courtesy of Nik Wheeler; pages 6-7: Stock Montage; pages 8, 9, 10-11: Nik Wheeler; pages 12, 32, 33: Ancient Art & Architecture Collection Ltd.; page 14: University of Pennsylvania Museum, Philadelphia (Neg. # S4-141589); pages 15, 37, 50: Louvre, Paris/Bridgeman Art Library Inernational, Ltd., London/New York; page 16: Kunsthistorisches Museum, Vienna/Bridgeman Art Library International, Ltd., London/New York; page 18-19: Private Collection/ Bridgeman Art Library International, Ltd., London/New York; page 22: Gallery A/Taos, NM; pages 24, 38 (top and bottom): British Museum, London/Bridgeman Art Library International, Ltd., London/New York; pages 26, 31, 45, 46, 51, 68: Louvre, Dpt. Des Antiquités Orientales, Paris/Erich Lessing/Art Resource, NY; page 29: British Museum, London/Erich Lessing/Art Resource, NY; pages 34-35: V. Southwell/Robert Harding Picture Library; page 36: Staatl Museen, Vorderasiatisches, Berlin, Germany/Erich Lessing/Art Resource, NY; page 39: Zev Radovan/BLMJ Borowski Collection; page 41: National Museum, Damascus, Syria/Giraudon/ Bridgeman Art Library International, Ltd., London/New York; page 44: British Library, London/Bridgeman Art Library International Ltd., London/New York; page 49: The Oriental Institute of the University of Chicago (P. 28752); page 52: Iraq Museum, Baghdad/Scala/Art Resource, NY; page 55: Richard Ashworth/Robert Harding Picture Library; page 57: The Granger Collection, New York; page 60-61: Chip Hires/Gamma Liaison; page 64: Louvre, Paris/Giraudon/Art Resource, NY; page 65: Bison Archives/Marc Wanamaker; page 67: Joseph Brignolo/The Image Bank; page 72: Marc Deville/Gamma Liaison

CONTENTS

CHAPTER ONE

THE CRADLE OF CIVILIZATION

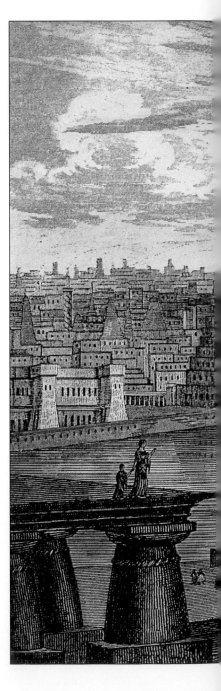

The ancient Greeks used the name *Mesopotamia* for a land whose civilization was even older than theirs. The name means "land between the rivers." Those rivers are the Euphrates and the Tigris, both of which flow southeast to the Persian Gulf through what is now Iraq.

The Greeks respected Mesopotamia for its old and rich culture. Today scholars know that this respect was well deserved and refer to Mesopotamia as the cradle of civilization. This was where humankind first began to live in cities and develop the complex type of culture that can be labeled "civilization."

Not only is the history of Mesopotamia long, it is also very complicated. Kingdoms and empires rose, fell, and rose again. Foreign conquerors came and went, often adopting the culture of the people they conquered. And through trade, military might, and the peaceful exchange of ideas, much of Mesopotamian culture spread throughout the world. Some influences can even be traced in the way we see and do things today.

Mesopotamia was important not simply as the cradle of civilization. For thousands of years it was also a hotbed of history—which, in some ways, it still is today.

In the Beginning

Most of Mesopotamia, away from its marshy rivers, is a flat, treeless plain, hot and dry with few natural resources. It doesn't seem a likely spot to give birth to civilization—and, in fact, ancient Mesopotamian culture began not on the plain but in the mountains north and east of the plain.

There green wooded hills enjoyed regular rainfall and supported a wide variety of plants and animals. The early people of the region were hunters and gatherers. They lived on game and wild plants, and they frequently had to move their homes to follow their food.

An artist's depiction of ancient Babylon, a walled, riverside city dominated by its many-layered temples, or ziggurats.

The Euphrates River near Baghdad, in modern Iraq.

Around 10,000 B.C.E.* they made a revolutionary change in their lives. Some people discovered that instead of eating all the wild seed they collected, they could plant some near their homes. Then food plants would grow there next season, and they wouldn't have to travel far to collect them. The people also discovered that they could have meat when they wanted it by protecting some of the wild herds from dangers and keeping them grazing nearby.

This change allowed people to build permanent homes and acquire more possessions. After a time, however, intense farming or grazing on the same land wore out the soil. These early farmers then began moving down into the Mesopotamian plain.

Here the soil was thick and rich, and it was kept that way by the yearly flooding of the Euphrates and Tigris Rivers. During the late spring these rivers, swollen by melting snow from the Taurus and Zagros Mountains, overflowed their banks, turning the whole plain into a lake. Retreating waters left behind rich soil carried down from the mountains.

*Many systems of dating have been used by different cultures throughout history. This series of books uses B.C.E. (Before Common Era) and C.E. (Common Era) instead of B.C. (Before Christ) and A.D. (Anno Domini) out of respect for the diversity of the world's peoples.

The early farmers learned that if they built villages on natural riverside levees or other higher ground, they could usually avoid being flooded out. When the waters receded, they could plant crops and graze animals in the fields nearby.

However, it seldom rained in the Mesopotamian plain. Frequently crops planted there dried up, until people discovered how to cut through the riverbanks and channel water into the fields to irrigate them. Planning, building, and maintaining a shared irrigation system was a complex task, beyond the abilities of a few individuals or families. It required community effort, and this gave rise to organized authorities, civil or religious leaders who could make decisions accepted by the group. People also needed authorities to decide the boundaries and ownership of farm fields and to settle disputes between landowners. And as the stable food supply of a village increased, so did its population and the need for more organization.

In southern Mesopotamia all these things led to another revolutionary change. Small, loosely organized villages evolved into structured cities. Civilization had begun.

The Marsh Arabs of modern Iraq live in much the same way as the early dwellers of Mesopotamia. They build their reed huts along the braided river channels, and they depend heavily on wild plants and animals.

Sumer, the First Civilization

The people who began that revolution in the sixth millennium B.C.E. were a mixed group. Some were farmers, originally from the mountains, who spoke a version of Sumerian. Others were nomadic herders who spoke a Semitic language and came from desert areas to the south and west. But by the time the civilization known as Sumer (SOOM-er) appeared, around 4300 B.C.E., all of southern Mesopotamia had a similar culture.

Sumer meant "plain" and was used for the area stretching from the Persian Gulf marshes to where the Euphrates and Tigris Rivers came closest together, near modern Baghdad, Iraq.

As the dozen or so cities in the area grew, they often found themselves in conflict over territory. When war broke out, the governing assemblies of each city chose a temporary leader to carry them through the crisis. But as wars became more constant, rulers became permanent and hereditary. Kingship had been born. Kings seemed more concerned about prestige and power than temporary leaders had been, and Sumerian history from around 3000 B.C.E. is largely one of cities fighting for control of their neighbors or of the entire region.

A Tale of Many Cities

In Mesopotamian mythology the first city to be created was Eridu, and archaeology supports this site's early claim. However, the first city to establish power over all of Sumer was Kish, possibly under a king named Etana. Next to dominate was the city of Uruk, one of whose kings was supposedly the legendary hero Gilgamesh. Other cities made bids for power, too, and centuries of civil war so weakened Sumer that it occasionally fell under the control of the Elamites, people from what is now southwestern Iran.

It was King Lugalannemandu of Adab who threw out the Elamites and won control of all

Sumer and some neighboring lands as well. After his death another period of civil war lasted until around 2450 B.C.E., when the city of Lagash rose to supreme power under King Eannatum. He first conquered the neighboring city of Umma, with which Lagash had fought over water rights. Several generations later Umma's king Lugalzagesi in turn destroyed Lagash and took control of most of Sumer and the important trade routes crossing through it. Lugalzagesi himself was defeated by another ambitious king and clapped into the stocks outside the city of Nippur, Sumer's most important religious center. This event, around 2350 B.C.E., marks the end of the early Dynastic Period of Sumerian history.

The ruins of ancient Uruk, a major city of Sumer and home of King Gilgamesh.

GILGAMESH, HISTORICAL HERO

The *Epic of Gilgamesh,* though an adventure tale of gods, monsters, and superhuman heroes, may also preserve some early Mesopotamian history. The prehistoric blending of farming and herding peoples may be remembered in the story's account of Enkidu, the wild man. First he lived free with the wild beasts; then he was tamed enough to help a group of herdsmen. Finally he was brought to a farming city where he fought, then joined, Gilgamesh, the king. Gilgamesh and Enkidu went on fantastic adventures, one of which may recall a historical Gilgamesh of Uruk sending expeditions to the mountains to bring back rare cedar for building the city's grand gates.

Here the epic tells of the two heroes meeting:

Mighty Gilgamesh came on, and Enkidu met him at the gate. He put out his foot and prevented Gilgamesh from entering the house, so they grappled, holding each other like bulls. They broke the doorposts and the walls shook, they snorted like bulls locked together. . . . Gilgamesh bent his knee with his foot planted on the ground and with a turn Enkidu was thrown. Then immediately his fury died.

When Enkidu was thrown, he said to Gilgamesh, "There is not another like you in the world. . . . Enlil [the chief god] has given you the kingship, for your strength surpasses the strength of men." So Enkidu and Gilgamesh embraced and their friendship was sealed.

The historical king Gilgamesh became a hero of popular legend. Scenes from the Gilgamesh epic were common in Mesopotamian art. Here the hero (at left) is shown giving water to a bull.

In the same way actual hunters, herders, and farmers sealed their joint history.

The king who defeated Lugalzagesi was Sargon the Great, one of the world's first empire builders. A legend about him was attached to several other Near Eastern leaders as well, including Moses of the Bible. As a baby Sargon was supposedly set adrift in a reed basket and was found and raised by someone who took him to the royal court. Sargon became an important official under the king of Kish but overthrew his ruler and made himself king.

He then set about bringing all of Mesopotamia, north and south, under his sway. Sargon's empire building carried him into parts of modern

Turkey, Syria, and Iran. The tribute and trade that poured into Sumer brought times of high prosperity.

Central Mesopotamia, from which Sargon came, was known as Akkad. Akkadian, a Semitic language, became the official language of government, and Sargon built himself a splendid new capital at Agade.

During his reign of fifty-six years, Sargon I was recorded as fighting thirty-four battles. He created new methods for governing, and during the reign of his grandson, Naram-sin (2254–2218 B.C.E.), the Akkadian Empire expanded. But rebellions and difficulty in governing so much territory weakened the empire, and it collapsed with the invasion of the Gutians, mountain people from the east, around 2220 B.C.E.

The Gutian destruction of the capital Agade was so total that even today archaeologists have not found its ruins. Attributing Agade's downfall to a curse of the gods, a Mesopotamian poet prophetically wrote, "May your clay [bricks] return to the depths of the earth. . . . May your palace built with a joyful heart be turned into a depressing ruin. . . . Over the place where your rites and rituals were conducted, may the fox who haunts the ruined mounds glide his tail."

The Last Days of Sumer

The Gutians ruled Sumer and Akkad for what was a century of economic and political collapse. The southern cities suffered less. At the end of the period, by around 2100 B.C.E., Gudea, the Sumerian ruler of Lagash, had enough wealth and independence to engage in massive building projects. But it was King Utuhegal of Uruk who finally threw the Gutians out. He was then overthrown by one of his generals, Ur-Nammu, who declared himself king of Ur around 2100 B.C.E. and set about building a smaller, more tightly administered version of Sargon's empire.

Under Ur-Nammu and his successors the economy prospered, Sumerian again became the official language, and there was a new flourishing of art and architecture. Ur-Nammu's son, Shulgi, was particularly praised by scribes for his many accomplishments, but this may have been partly due to his funding of two new schools for scribes.

But again prosperity was its own undoing. Attracted to the wealth of Sumer, Amorites (Semitic nomads) began moving in from the west, weakening imperial control. Taking advantage of this, the Elamites

The excavations of Leonard Woolley (foreground, second from left) *at Ur revealed a thick deposit of water-born clay. Woolley believed this was left by the flood recorded in Sumerian legends and in the Bible.*

attacked from the east, destroying Ur around 2000 B.C.E. and closing the Sumerian chapter of Mesopotamian history.

Fabled Babylon

Though partly responsible for the decline of Sumer, the Amorites had for years been settling down and adopting Mesopotamian ways. Many Amorites had become political leaders as well, and they, too, accepted the government system, religion, art, and architecture of their adopted land. For two centuries Amorite kings of Larsa and Isin were the major powers in Mesopotamia.

In 1894 B.C.E. an Amorite chieftain, Sumu-abum, made himself king of Babylon, a small city in central Mesopotamia. He and his successors spent their reigns improving the economy, irrigation, public buildings, and administration of their city-state. When Hammurabi came to the throne of Babylon in 1792 B.C.E., he built on this foundation, establishing a code of laws and involving himself in all aspects of running the city.

Hammurabi's interests also extended beyond his borders, and he skillfully built military and diplomatic alliances with his neighbors. In the thirty-first year of his reign he turned to military conquest; attacked cities in the south, west, and north; and unified all of Mesopotamia under a Babylonian empire.

Babylon's diplomatic and trade contacts reached west to the Mediterranean Sea. Akkadian and its cuneiform writing system became the language of commerce and diplomacy throughout much of the ancient world. At home, Babylonian, a version of Akkadian, had become the language of government, but Sumerian was still used for religious writing. The government system, arts, and architecture remained basically Sumerian, as did the religion, although the names of the deities changed.

This first Babylonian empire did not long survive its founder, and by the time Hammurabi's dynasty came to an end, Babylonia had shrunk to around fifty square miles. The death-blow was dealt by the Hittites, a militant new kingdom in what is now Turkey. In 1595 B.C.E. they swept into Babylonia, burned and looted its capital, then returned to their northern mountains.

Babylon then fell under the control of the Kassites, who may originally have been mountain people. Kassite dynasties ruled Babylon for four hundred prosperous years. They made a point of fully adopting Mesopotamia's culture, and they expanded into an empire almost as large as Hammurabi's. Kassite Babylon exchanged ambassadors with Egypt, and the royal families of the two distant kingdoms even intermarried.

In 1171 B.C.E. Mesopotamia's old enemy on the east, Elam, attacked Babylon. Elamites looted the city and carried off the sacred statue of the city's special god, Marduk. An unsettled period followed for Babylon under the rule of six local dynasties.

This statue is kneeling in prayer for the health of King Hammurabi. Of bronze and gold, the figure dates from around 1750 B.C.E. and was found in southern Mesopotamia.

Construction of the Tower of Babel has long been a favorite subject for artists. The biblical account probably referred to Mesopotamian ziggurats, particularly Babylon's Marduk temple. This painting was done by Flemish artist Pieter Brueghel in 1563.

At one point, Nebuchadrezzar I (reigned 1124–1103 B.C.E.) led a surprise attack on Elam during the hottest period of summer and carried the statue of Marduk back home. But even with its god returned, Babylon entered a long period of decline. Power in Mesopotamia had now shifted to the north.

Assyria, Power of the North

Northern Mesopotamia was less intensely urbanized than the south because seasonal rainfall allowed the survival of small nonirrigated communities. The city of Ashur was established under a king around 2500 B.C.E. For centuries instead of a political empire it built extensive regional trade routes and protected these by frequently fighting tribes from the Zagros Mountains. During the course of time Ashur was part of the empires of Akkad, Ur, and Babylon.

The first ruler of Assyria with imperial ideas was Shamshi-Adad, an Amorite military leader. Around 1810 B.C.E. he made himself king of

WAR PROPAGANDA

Assyrian kings waged almost continuous warfare against their neighbors and rebellious subjects. They recorded their campaigns in great detail on clay tablets and stone monuments, putting particular stress on their might and ruthlessness. They did so not just to preserve history but also to impress people with the foolishness of resisting Assyria. If cities paid their tribute, Assyrian kings would not flay their leaders, tacking their skins on the city gates, and Assyrian armies would not fill the wide plains with their enemies' corpses and "dye the mountain like red wool" with their blood.

All of the royal annals seem boastfully bloodthirsty, but that of Ashurnasirpal is perhaps the most wordy. In the fifth year of his reign the "great king, the mighty king, king of the universe, king of Assyria" records a series of conquests including the following:

Chariots and picked cavalry I took with me, and on rafts I crossed the Tigris. All night I marched and I drew nigh unto Pitura, the stronghold of the men of Dirra. The city was exceedingly strong and was surrounded by two walls. Its citadel was like a mountain peak. With the supreme might of Ashur, my lord, with the multitude of my hosts and with my furious battle onslaught I fought with them. For two days, from before sunrise, I thundered against them like Agad [the god] of the storm, and I rained down flame upon them. With courage and might, my warriors flew against them like Zu [the Storm Bird]. I took the city, and eight hundred of their fighting men I put to the sword, and cut off their heads. Multitudes I captured alive, and the rest of them I burned with fire, and carried off their heavy spoil. I formed a pillar of the living and a pillar of heads against the city gate, and seven hundred men I impaled on stakes over against their city gate. The city, I destroyed, I devastated and I turned it into a mound and ruin heap. Their young men and their maidens I burned in the fire.

Actually the Assyrian army, though ruthless, was probably not much more so than others of its time. But it was among the most effective at using this reputation as war propaganda. It's not surprising that, hearing stories like this, many cities gave in and paid their tribute.

Assyria and came to control most of northern Mesopotamia as well as parts of modern Syria and Turkey. After his death the empire dwindled, and with the rise of Hammurabi to the south, Assyria fell briefly under Babylonian rule.

The decline of Babylonia didn't help Assyria because around 1500 B.C.E. it was conquered by Mitanni, a kingdom to its northwest. Regaining its independence 150 years later, Assyria engaged in years of up-and-down conflict with Babylon and other neighbors. At times it ruled a military empire with extensive diplomatic ties around the region.

At this time the whole Near East was experiencing population movements, possibly because of a long period of drought. For Mesopotamia this meant another incursion of nomads from the western deserts, the Arameans. Assyrian king Tiglath-Pileser I spent much of his reign driving back Arameans, reopening trade routes they had cut, and expanding into neighboring territories. He did so with a military strength and a ruthless efficiency that made the Assyrians feared for many centuries to come.

The main aims of his conquests seem to have been trade, tribute, and booty, and he did not follow up with effective imperial government. At Tiglath-Pileser's death in 1077 B.C.E., his empire collapsed. Arameans continued to plague Assyria for a century and established a few minor kingdoms of their own.

Imperial Assyria

In 934 B.C.E. there arose a line of kings who strengthened Assyria's government and economy, then turned to empire building. Theirs was an impressive military. Professional soldiers, hardened by years of conflict with Arameans and others, were equipped with two relatively new military advances. From the north they had learned about iron weapons as well as the use of horses for cavalry and as a means of pulling chariots. They perfected the tactics of siege warfare and of deporting whole populations from conquered territories. By using foot soldiers, archers, chariots, and siege equipment all at the same time, Assyrian armies had a great advantage over opponents using single techniques.

The greatest of this line, Ashurnasirpal II (reigned 883–859 B.C.E.), conquered Aramean cities, reclaimed rebellious territories, established military outposts, expanded into new areas, and built himself a new

capital at Kalhu. He and his son drove the Assyrian war machine west to the Mediterranean and won the submission of numerous kindgoms, including Israel.

These kings, like earlier Assyrian imperialists, ran their military expeditions largely to destroy enemies, strike terror into neighbors, and bring back booty and tribute. This approach poured wealth into Assyria but did not secure well-run, long-lasting empires. In time conquered provinces rebelled and the empire declined.

The Assyrian royal palace at Nimrud in the seventh century B.C.E., as imagined by a nineteenth-century artist.

In 744 B.C.E. King Tiglath-Pileser III (called Pul in the Bible) began placing the Assyrian Empire on new footing. Internal reforms secured his control at home. He reorganized the army, instituted a spy network, tightened control over conquered territories, and began the world's first postal system, with runners who carried reports to and from the far-flung reaches of the empire.

Sargon II spent his reign putting down rebellions and expanding into new territory. He led a spectacular raid through the Zagros Mountains into Urartu, and spent much of his wealth in building a grand new capital at Dur-Sharrukin. At his death new rebellions broke out, but his successor, Sennacherib (reigned 704–681 B.C.E.), ruthlessly crushed them. Sennacherib's destruction of rebellious but revered Babylon shocked many of his people. He was supposedly killed at his new capital of Nineveh by one of his own sons, who beat him with a statue looted from Babylon.

Another son, Esarhaddon, took the throne and rebuilt Babylon. Later he and then his son Assurbanipal II (reigned 668–627 B.C.E.) attacked Egypt. For a short time the Assyrian Empire extended from the Nile River and the Mediterranean Sea on the west, through modern Turkey and Iran, and south to the Persian Gulf.

This was the largest empire the world had yet known, but it had sown the seeds of its own destruction. It was too large to control or defend, its soldiers were exhausted after years of warfare, and its policies of mass slaughter and deportation had created deep hatred for Assyria. Rebellions spread like wildfire. The Medes attacked from the east and Babylon from the south. By 612 B.C.E. the grand empire had vanished, and its cities in the heart of Assyria were reduced to smoking ruins.

The Last Glories of Babylon

At the time of Assyria's fall, Babylon was run by a dynasty of Chaldeans, another nomadic people who had become totally Mesopotamian. In 605 B.C.E. the last of Assyria's forces and their Egyptian allies met Babylon in battle at Carchemish (KAR-kuh-mish). The Babylonians under Prince Nebuchadrezzar were victorious, and shortly afterward the throne went to this general, King Nebuchadrezzar II.

Babylon considered that it had inherited much of Assyria's empire, and Nebuchadrezzar spent some time putting down rebellions and fighting

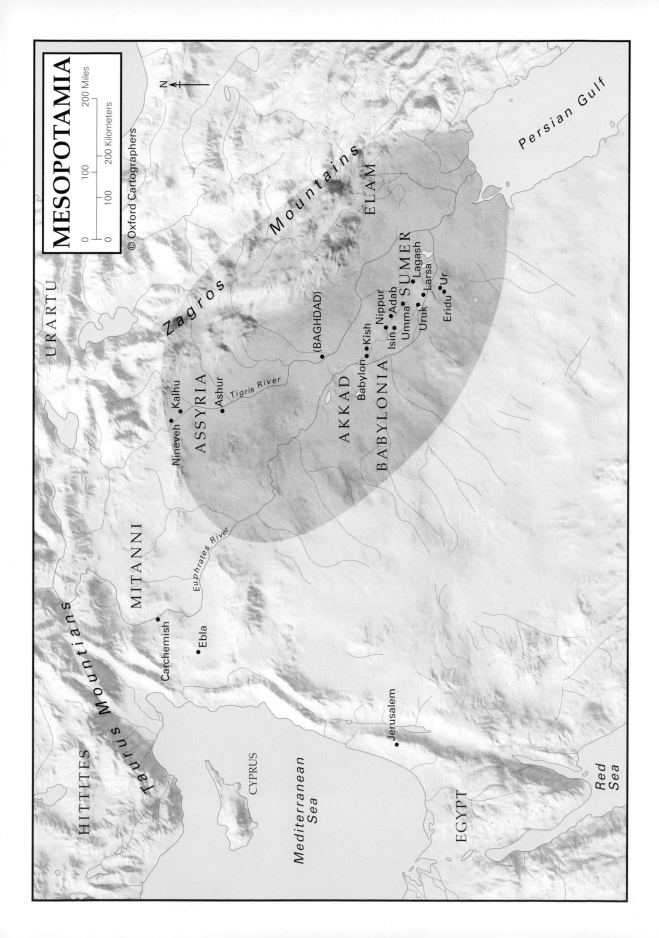

MESOPOTAMIA

200 Miles

200 Kilometers

100

100

© Oxford Cartographers

N

Persian Gulf

URARTU

Zagros Mountains

ELAM

SUMER

Nippur
Adab
Isin Umma Lagash
Kish Uruk Larsa
Babylon Eridu Ur

(BAGHDAD)

ASSYRIA

Nineveh Kalhu
Ashur

Tigris River

AKKAD

BABYLONIA

Euphrates River

MITANNI

Carchemish

Ebla

HITTITES

Taurus Mountains

CYPRUS

Mediterranean Sea

Jerusalem

EGYPT

Red Sea

The Hanging Gardens of Babylon were built in stone terraces that climbed one above the other until they rose, like a mountain, high above the magnificent city. This painting is an artist's idea of the way the city and gardens looked.

off Egypt. The Bible records how he destroyed Jerusalem and deported its people to Babylon.

Most of Nebuchadrezzar II's reign, from 605–562 B.C.E., however, focused on returning Babylonia to its former glory. Several ancient Sumerian cities, devastated by years of warfare, were restored, and Babylon was fortified and rebuilt in a spectacular way. The city's beautiful terraced gardens, which Nebuchadrezzar built to make his wife Amyitis less homesick for her mountain homeland, became famous as The Hanging Gardens of Babylon, one of the seven wonders of the ancient world. The rebuilt temple of the god Marduk rose 650 feet into the Babylonian sky and may have inspired the Bibles' account of the Tower of Babel. No doubt exiled Hebrew slaves had a part in its construction.

The seventy-five years of Babylon's Chaldean restoration were prosperous ones for Mesopotamia, but this was to prove the last period in Mesopotamia's long history as an independent power.

Across the mountains to the east, in what is now Iran, the Persians had been building an empire of their own. Cyrus, their king, had conquered territory extending from Greece to India. In 539 B.C.E. during the sacred New Year's festival, Cyrus attacked and captured Babylon. All of Mesopotamia became part of the Persian Empire. The independent history of this ancient land, the cradle of civilization, had come to an end.

CHAPTER TWO

LIFE BETWEEN THE RIVERS

The Beginning of Writing

It has been said that "history begins at Sumer." Of course important events happened before the time of Sumer, but the difference between history and prehistory is that history is written down. In developing a system of writing, the people of Mesopotamia were the first to make history possible.

Mesopotamians didn't begin to write because they wanted to preserve history. They had more practical things in mind. They were involved in commerce from early on and needed a way to keep track of how many cattle or sacks of grain they sold.

Mesopotamia had few trees or papyrus plants for making paper, but one thing it did have was plenty of mud. People made tablets of wet clay and scratched pictures on them to show objects

The Royal Standard of Ur is a mosaic panel found in a magnificent Sumerian tomb. This side shows offerings being brought to the king and members of his court while they drink wine and are entertained by a harpist. The other side shows scenes of warfare.

FROM PICTURES TO WRITING

The development of Mesopotamian writing can be traced from simple pictures to complex cuneiform.

	A Original pictograph	B Pictograph in position of later cuneiform	C Early Babylonian	D Assyrian	E Original or derived meaning
1					bird
2					fish
3					donkey
4					ox
5					sun day
6					grain
7					orchard
8					to plow to till
9					boomerang to throw to throw down
10					to stand to go

and numbers. The earliest clay tablets found so far are from the city of Uruk around 3100 B.C.E.

Soon people wanted to write down more complicated things, so they began using pictures to represent the sounds of words in Sumerian. These sound signs could then be combined to make new words. Sometimes the Sumerians used a picture to show a related meaning. A drawing of a head

This Sumerian clay tablet is about five thousand years old and is an example of an early form of writing using pictures. Picture writing later developed into the wedge-shaped marks of cuneiform.

could mean "head," or it could stand for the sound *sag,* which was "head" in Sumerian, or it could also mean "to think."

Originally these signs were drawn upright with a pointed reed. Then they were turned sideways to avoid smearing the wet clay, and gradually the pictures became a nonrealistic pattern of short lines. Finally a stylus with a wedge-shaped point was used to imprint these lines. This writing system is now called cuneiform from the Latin for "wedge-shaped."

Though not fully alphabetic like our writing system, cuneiform was adapted for use with Akkadian, Babylonian, Persian, and other languages. The first major Mesopotamian empire, the Akkadian, spread the use of cuneiform and the Akkadian language until this became the common language of commerce and diplomacy in much of the ancient Near East. And although clay tablets were less portable than paper or papyrus, records kept on them lasted in great numbers for thousands of years, particularly if the tablets were fired in a kiln or accidentally fired when a town was burned. Many of the records of people who wrote in more destructible materials have been lost forever.

Early Schools

Learning to write cuneiform was hard work. Over two thousand signs had to be memorized, the neat inscribing of tiny marks had to be practiced, and proper grammar and style had to be developed. In Babylonian and Assyrian times, when Sumerian was used for religious writing but not for everyday speech, learning to write could also mean learning a second language.

To teach all this, schools for scribes, or "tablet houses," were founded. There sons of wealthier families studied from the time they were young boys until they were men. Girls generally did not attend school, although some might be taught privately. Princess Enheduanna, daughter of Sargon the Great, was known as a gifted poet.

Scribe schools also became the centers for other kinds of learning, because in studying writing, students copied all sorts of texts, including king lists, lists of different types of animals and plants, mathematical works, and pieces of literature. Sometimes the only surviving copies of these works are ones that were made by schoolboys.

These boys attended school daily from sunrise to sunset and spent their days copying texts, reciting lessons, and listening to lectures by their teachers, or "big brothers" as they were called. Discipline was strict, and students were readily caned for being late, doing poor work, talking, and other offenses.

Not all boys took well to school. One surviving dialogue records a father, himself a scribe, complaining that his son doesn't appreciate being sent to a scribe school instead of having to do physical labor like other boys.

Annoyed over the boy's truancy, the father asks, "Where did you go?"

"I did not go anywhere."

"If you did not go anywhere, why do you idle about? Go to school and stand before your 'school father' [principal], recite your assignment, open your school bag, write your tablet, let your 'big brother' write your new tablet for you. After you have finished your assignment and reported to your monitor, come to me and do not wander about in the street."

We do not know if this schoolboy ever took his father's advice, but if he did, he would probably have become an important person in his society. Most Mesopotamians could not read, and scribes were needed in almost every area of life. Illiterate merchants, priests, judges, generals, and even kings needed scribes to write and read messages and to keep records. Mesopotamian schools may have been hard, but they almost guaranteed their graduates a job.

WORDS TO THE WISE

A type of literature common in the ancient Near East was made up of proverbs, or wise sayings. This sampling from Mesopotamia shows that despite the centuries, people haven't changed much.

*Who possesses much silver may
   be happy,
Who possesses much grain may
   be glad,
But he who has nothing can sleep.*

❖

Friendship lasts a day, kinship forever.

❖

*For a man's pleasure, there is marriage;
On thinking it over, there is divorce.*

❖

*If you take the field of an enemy,
The enemy will come and take
   your field.*

❖

*We are doomed to die; let us spend.
We will live long; let us save.*

*He who leaves the fight unfinished is
   not at peace.*

❖

*He did not yet catch the fox,
Yet he is making a collar for it.*

❖

*Upon my escaping the wild ox,
The wild cow confronted me.*

❖

*Tell a lie; then if you tell the truth,
It will be deemed a lie.*

❖

*You can have a lord, you can have
   a king,
But the man to fear is the tax
   collector!*

The ass was the main pack animal throughout Mesopotamian history. Here hunting gear is being carried by an ass in a relief carving on the walls of Assurbanipal II's palace at Nineveh.

A Living from the Soil

Mesopotamia grew rich through commerce and grew powerful through conquests, but the basis of its life was farming. Wheat, barley, and millet, domesticated from local wild varieties, were the main food crops. Palms gave sweet dates, and other trees were planted for their fruit and to provide shaded gardens. There, vegetables such as cucumbers, onions, and lettuce could grow shielded from the scorching Mesopotamian sun.

Cattle, sheep, goats, and pigs, also domesticated from types found locally in the wild, provided meat, leather, milk, and wool. Oxen and asses were the main beasts of burden, with horses only arriving in Assyrian times. Hunting and fishing in the marshes provided additional food.

Since the Mesopotamians were so keen on writing everything down, it's not surprising that the world's first farmer's almanac was found on a Sumerian tablet over thirty-five hundred years old. It lays out instructions on how to irrigate, when to plant, how deep to plant different seeds, and when to harvest. Even though the instructions for keeping away field mice are to pray to Ninkilim, goddess of vermin, the almanac is mostly full of sound practical advice based on years of experience.

The technology behind Mesopotamian farming was surprisingly advanced. Farmers used one type of ox-pulled plow to break up the soil and another type both to dig a furrow and to drop in seeds. The complex irrigation system not only involved digging and repairing canals, it also used bucket-lifting devices to move water between levels. Whenever political troubles disrupted the irrigation systems, bad times of hunger and social disaster usually followed.

Other problems faced farmers as well. Sometimes the winters dropped so little snow in the mountains that the spring floods were very poor, and the crops failed. At other times the floods rose so high that towns were nearly destroyed. Also, river channels tended to change over time, and a town built beside a river might find itself far from water several centuries later. Some of the historical rise and fall of Mesopotamian cities came as much from shifting rivers as from shifting politics.

Another problem was that after the same farm fields had been irrigated for years, the soil became more and more salty, and crops don't grow well in salty soil. This may be one reason why political and economic power shifted northward in Mesopotamia—away from Sumer, where the soils had been farmed longest.

Center of Commerce

Farmers fed the cities of Mesopotamia, but the wealth of the cities rose from their merchants and craftspeople. The Mesopotamians placed great value on commerce. Material success was seen as a prime goal in life and a sign of the gods' favor.

Mesopotamia was poor in natural resources such as metal, timber, and stone. Even in prehistoric times Mesopotamians imported obsidian and other stone for making tools. Copper, the metal that ended the Stone Age, came from the north at least by 6500 B.C.E.

Goods were carried up and down Mesopotamia's two rivers in boats made of skin-covered reeds. More substantial merchant galleys sailed the Red Sea, the Mediterranean, and the Persian Gulf, and donkey caravans traveled extensive overland trade routes. Goods came to Mesopotamia from as far away as Africa, Europe, India, and from most points between.

Wood was a valued trade item in treeless Mesopotamia. This relief from the palace of Assyria's king Sargon shows cedar logs being unloaded from a boat.

What Mesopotamia gave in exchange was mostly grain and textiles. But once the imported stone, metal, or wood reached Mesopotamia, craftspeople made tools, jewelry, and other objects that could then be traded.

Coins weren't used in ancient Mesopotamia, but after a time standards based on the weight of silver or grain were established. A person might give so many silver units worth of cloth in exchange for an equal value of leather work or cucumbers.

Control of trade routes was one of the frequent issues in warfare between Mesopotamian cities, and this control was a major aim of Mesopotamia's empire builders. Kings regularly boasted of all the fine woods, stone, and other foreign luxuries glorifying their palaces.

Layers of Society

The kings and their families were at the top of Mesopotamian society, but beneath them were many other levels, none of them absolutely rigid.

The most powerful and wealthy group was made up of the large landowners and the top ranks of the government, military, and priesthoods. Below them came the merchants, scribes, and all the various craftspeople, many of whom were organized into guilds. The numbers of independent small farmers, hunters, and herders decreased over time, but the ranks of professional soldiers increased. As more land and property came to be owned by wealthy families, temples, or the king, more people became laborers working for others.

Slaves were on the lowest social rung. These were foreign captives or locals who had fallen into slavery because of debt or because they had been sold as children by impoverished parents.

This elaborate headdress and jewelry, made of gold and semiprecious stones, shows the great wealth of Mesopotamian royalty and the skill of their metalworkers. It was worn by Queen Pu Abi, who was buried at Ur around 2500 B.C.E.

Foreign slaves were traded into Mesopotamia as were other commodities.

This whole structure was somewhat flexible. A clever scribe might rise to a position of power in government, and the wealthier a merchant became, the more influence he was likely to have. A man from a humble background might become king if he was strong and clever enough to overthrow the previous king. Even slaves could own property, engage in business, and eventually buy their freedom.

Still, Mesopotamian society was generally one in which people knew their places and stayed there. Sons were usually expected to follow their father's trade, and daughters had few opportunities to follow any trade at all. Women did have some rights, particularly in Sumerian times. They could own property, engage in business, and hold positions of power as priestesses. In government their role was usually limited to whatever personal influence they might have over the men in power. No queens ruled in their own right, although some acted as regents while their sons were underage or away at war.

This relief carving of a scribe holding a clay tablet and stylus is from the Assyrian palace at Nineveh around 640 B.C.E.

Greatness Built from Mud

Mesopotamian architects achieved great things, but the remains of their structures discovered in recent times have made less of an impression on the public than have the buildings of other ancient cultures. The basic Mesopotamian building material was mud brick, not the lasting stone of Egypt's pyramids or Greece's columned temples.

Mesopotamia's earliest inhabitants sometimes lived in round homes or in reed huts plastered with mud. By early Sumerian times the architectural styles and techniques for the next three thousand years had been established.

Mud was shaped into rectangular bricks, which in early days were humped on top like loaves of bread. Mud or bitumen, a natural tar, was used as plaster. Wealthier people sometimes used bricks hardened by fire, but most bricks were simply dried in the sun. After a time these bricks would melt or crumble, and when repair became too much trouble, buildings were abandoned or torn down and new ones built on top. This meant that the remains of older towns became hills under the newer ones. These occupation mounds, called tells, still dot the region.

The towns, surrounded by defensive walls, grew haphazardly in a maze of winding unpaved lanes, though wide cobbled roads were built near the temples and palaces. Open areas used as markets were not only the centers of economic activity, but also meeting places where people exchanged news. Sometimes kings rebuilt old cities on grander, more organized lines or erected brand-new cities with streets laid out in grids.

Towns often had elaborate drainage systems with clay pipes lined with bitumen, and some homes even had flush toilets. Towns did not, however, have garbage collection systems, and rubbish was just thrown into the streets. Street levels built up so high that steps had to be cut down from the streets to the front doors until eventually new houses were constructed over the remains of the old.

Homes were usually square or rectangular, with rooms built around an open courtyard. Wealthier homes had two stories, with balconies on the top floor. Palm logs plastered with mud formed the roofs.

In narrow courtyards behind the houses, shrines were built for the family's gods, and sometimes dead family members were buried under the pavement. Furniture was fairly simple, and even in wealthy homes people often squatted on the floor or sat on rugs or pillows.

In order to keep out the fierce Mesopotamian heat, the walls of private homes, temples, and palaces were thick, whitewashed, and had no

windows. The doors in houses were usually low for the same reason, though in public buildings the demands of dignity raised doorways above stooping levels.

In other ways, too, temples and palaces were far grander. They could cover many acres and were almost small cities, having their own cooks, cloth makers, metalworkers, scribes, guards, and

The homes of modern Iraqi Marsh Arabs are very similar to those of marsh dwellers shown in ancient Mesopotamian art. The banded designs and columns of bound reeds were architectural details carried over in later Mesopotamian brick buildings.

The enameled tiles on Babylon's Ishtar Gate depict real and mythical beasts. Designed to awe the subjects of Nebuchadrezzar II, they now impress visitors to a museum in Berlin.

armies of servants. And they were splendidly decorated. The columns and windowless walls of grand Sumerian buildings were often covered with mosaics made by sticking painted clay pegs into the building clay. In Babylonian and Assyrian times brilliantly colored glazed bricks decorated palace and temple walls, impressing the public with the grandeur of the gods and king. In all periods plastered walls might be painted with pictures or designs, and stone relief carvings were particularly popular in later times.

Art to Please People and Gods

From the beginning, art was a way people expressed their understanding of life and their pleasure in it. Assuming that whatever they enjoyed, their deities would enjoy as well, the Mesopotamians worked art into every part of their lives, from the way they worshiped to the pots they cooked in and the furniture they used daily. Many of their works of art have been lost to time, but enough have survived to show that the Mesopotamians were a talented people with a strong sense of life's beauty.

Today the Sumerians and pre-Sumerians are especially known for their sculptures, particularly the figures of worshipers, which were first made in clay and then in stone. The figures, stylized at first and then becoming more naturalistic, were done in a very distinctive way. In contrast to the cool, slender grace of ancient Egyptian figures, for example, the human figures made by Sumerian artists were solid and squat with large, trusting eyes and hopeful, friendly smiles.

In Babylonian and Assyrian times wall paintings and reliefs became more important than freestanding sculptures. These new works, however, had many similarities in style to the old. Great attention, for example, was paid to details, such as the changing fashions in hair and clothing. But whereas the earlier figures were intended to appeal to the gods, the relief carvings of later times were meant to impress people with the power and majesty of their gods and kings. The friendly, simple look was gone.

Assyrian kings commemorated military victories, temple construction, and their hunting prowess on vases, wall plaques, stone slabs, palace walls, and even carved into the rock of mountainsides. A few of the colossal winged beasts that guarded Assyrian gateways are now in museums, where they still awe people.

Not all Mesopotamian artwork was sacred or monumental. Pottery, even for everyday use, was often well made and decorated. Pottery styles changed frequently enough so that broken pieces are a good way to date archaeological sites.

Metalworking was another important Mesopotamian art form. Because metal had to be imported, however, the fine products made from it were usually enjoyed only by the wealthy. Copper

The Persians, neighbors and finally conquerors of Mesopotamia, adopted many Mesopotamian art styles. This winged bull in enameled tiles is from Susa in Persia around 500 B.C.E.

This bullheaded lyre dates from 2500 B.C.E. and is one of the world's earliest examples of fine metalwork. Note the similarity between this harp and the one shown on the Royal Standard of Ur on page 24.

was used as early as the seventh millennium B.C.E., and during Sumerian times gold, silver, and bronze appeared as well. Even ordinary metal objects such as weapons, cups, and bridles might be beautifully decorated. And among the most exquisite uses of gold known from the ancient world are the standing goat statues, the decorated harp, and the elaborate jewelry found in the Royal Cemetery of Ur.

The metal that had the biggest impact on Mesopotamian history was iron. It was introduced to Assyria probably by the Hittites. Being far stronger than other metals, it made excellent tools and weapons. Use of iron weapons gave the Assyrian armies an advantage in spreading their empire. Iron was harder to work than other metals, and being a less attractive color, had fewer uses in art.

Inlaying was another technique in which Mesopotamian artists excelled, possibly because they seldom had large amounts of valuable materials to work with. Tiny pieces of metal, gems, stone, ivory, or glass were set into other material using bitumen as a glue. A variety of objects were decorated this way, including furniture, jewelry, musical instruments, boxes, and gaming boards.

Finally, there is that most "typically Mesopotamian" object, the cylinder seal, which combines this culture's focus on commerce with its eye for artistic beauty and detail. Thousands of these seals have been found in Mesopotamian sites, and their

Inlaying was a detailed art, perfected in the Sumerian period. This gaming board, inlaid with tiny pieces of shell and stone, entertained members of the royal household of Ur during their lives and accompanied them in death.

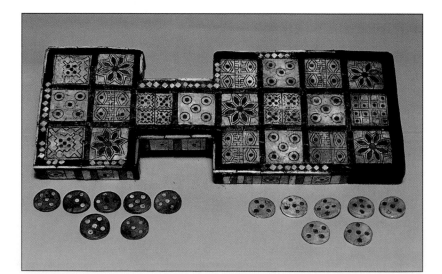

discovery elsewhere is a sign of Mesopotamian involvement throughout the ancient Near East.

The cylinders, an inch or so long, were usually carved out of stone. They had holes down the center for stringing and were carved with inset designs so that when rolled on wet clay they left a raised pattern on the surface. Cylinder seals served as personal signatures. Merchants might use them to mark shipments of goods as theirs, and government and temple officials used them to officially stamp documents.

Artists specializing in carving seals used a number of stock designs and others specially ordered by customers. Different types of designs were popular at different times and with different groups. Some seals showed animals and plants, while others depicted religious ceremonies or scenes from mythology. Still others showed battle and hunting scenes. When worn, no doubt they were seen not only as beautiful and useful objects, but as status symbols, showing that this person was important enough to need to identify things as being his.

Once again art appears in a very practical, Mesopotamian way.

The cylinder seal, when rolled in wet clay, left its carved pattern in reverse as an identification of the owner. Mesopotamian artists lavished great skill and detail on these practical objects.

CHAPTER THREE LAND OF GODS AND DEMONS

No doubt human beings have always wondered about life and our role in it. Some form of religious belief seems to have been with us from the start. But it was the people of Mesopotamia who first wrote down their beliefs. These records, plus the archaeological evidence, give a picture of a complex religion that guided Mesopotamian lives for several thousand years.

The religion of Sumer probably reflected a blending of many earlier beliefs. A farming society where women and a fertility goddess were important combined with a nomadic herding society dominated by men and male gods.

Each settlement had its own patron deities, and as different cities rose and fell in power, the gods linked with those cities changed in importance. Over time some similar deities were combined, and with political changes often the divine names changed as well. However, from Sumerian through Babylonian and Assyrian times, the basic beliefs and collection of deities stayed much the same.

Mesopotamia was a land always threatened with uncertainty. Floods that were too low or too high could spell disaster. Insects, plagues, or terrible dust storms could sweep the land, and enemies seemed to lurk in nearby deserts or mountains.

It's not surprising, then, that Mesopotamians looked for order and pattern in the world and that they hoped to work within the pattern to try to change a few things in their favor.

The Mesopotamians saw their universe as peopled by thousands of supernatural beings, who ranged from controllers of nature to supervisors of every detail of daily life. There were demons, too, both good and bad, and every person had his or her own divine guardian. All of these divinities were powerful, mysterious, and a little frightening, just the way life seemed to be. But they were enough like humans, with the same needs and weaknesses, to be somewhat understood and possibly even to be open to influence.

40

Inanna, later called Ishtar, was the goddess of both love and war. This female figure, with her special headdress and large eyes, may have been a priestess of Inanna.

The Creation

Mesopotamian beliefs about the creation and early days of the world are in many ways similar to those held elsewhere around the ancient Near East and Mediterranean. Some of this similarity can be traced to Mesopotamian influence on other regions, but some may come from beliefs held in common over a wide area. Certainly many stories told in the Bible echo those from Mesopotamia.

There were several versions of the Mesopotamian creation

myth, but basically it says that in the beginning there was watery chaos ruled by the god of freshwater and the goddess of salt water. They created other deities by naming them, and eventually the sky god An (or Anu) appeared. He supplanted the earlier gods and goddesses and set about creation on his own. Enlil, god of air, separated An from Ninhursag, Mother Earth, and Enki (or Ea) became god of wisdom and subterranean waters. Shamash, god of the sun, and Nammu Sin, god of the moon, provided light, while Inanna (Ishtar in Assyrian and Babylonian times) became goddess of love and of war. She, like the later Roman goddess of love, was identified with the planet Venus.

These and many other deities presided over a world that was conceived of as a flat disk, with a Netherworld tucked underneath, that floated between ocean and sky. The deities created plants and animals and built a special paradise for themselves: Dilmun, the Mesopotamian Garden of Eden. Here one of the gods got into trouble for eating forbidden plants, and goddesses were created to cure him, one being made from his rib.

In time, most of the gods and goddesses grew tired of having to tend to everything themselves. They even went on strike and refused to dig any more irrigation canals, so a god molded humans out of clay, giving them life with his breath or, in some versions, with divine blood. The role of humans was to serve the needs of the gods, and Enki taught them farming and other skills so they could do this. Paradise and immortality, however, remained reserved for the gods.

The Flood

Humanity began to multiply, and after a time there were so many people, making so much noise, that the divine council, headed by Enlil, decided to destroy them with a flood. Enki, however, always a friend of humankind, secretly warned a Sumerian king, Utnapishtim (or Zinsudra) by talking to a reed wall that he knew Utnapishtim was hiding behind. Enki gave detailed instructions for building a huge boat with six decks in which Utnapishtim, his family, retainers, livestock, and wild beasts could be saved.

After the boat was ready, a terrible storm broke out that destroyed everything on earth and even frightened the gods and goddesses. On the seventh day the ship landed on a mountain and Utnapishtim sent out birds to see if it was safe to release his passengers. He then offered a sacrifice

UTNAPISHTIM'S ARK: EXCERPTS FROM THE MESOPOTAMIAN FLOOD STORY

Enki said secretly to Utnapishtim: "Give up possessions, seek life. Foreswear worldly goods, and keep the soul alive. Aboard the ship, take the seed of all living things. The ship that you build, her dimensions shall be to measure."

So Utnapishtim and his retainers built the ship six decks high, sealed it with bitumen, and provisioned it. When all were inside, the hatch was closed.

"With the first glow of dawn, a black cloud rose up from the horizon. . . . The wide land was shattered like a pot. For one day the storm wind blew, gathering speed as it blew, submerging the mountains, overtaking the people like a battle. No one can see his fellow nor can the people be recognized from heaven."

The gods and goddesses, in fact, were so frightened that they scurried up to heaven, where they cowered "like dogs crouching against the outer wall." On the seventh day the storm subsided, and Utnapishtim looked out.

"I looked at the weather; stillness had set in, and all of mankind had returned to clay. The landscape was as level as a flat roof. I opened a hatch and light fell on my face. I looked about for the coastline in the expanse of sea. Bowing low, I wept."

Landing on Mount Nitsir, Utnapishtim "sent forth and set free a dove. The dove went forth but came back since no resting place for it was visible." Later he had the same results with a swallow. "Then, I sent forth and set free a raven. The raven went forth and seeing that the water had diminished, he eats, circles, caws and turns not around.

"Then I let out all to the four winds and offered a sacrifice. I poured out a libation on the top of the mountain. . . . The gods smelled the sweet savor. The gods crowded like flies about the sacrificer."

In ancient Mesopotamia, humankind and the divine were reconciled again.

to the gods, which the goddess Ishtar angrily told Enlil he didn't deserve because the flood had been his idea in the first place. She then swore on her jeweled necklace, the rainbow, that the gods wouldn't destroy humankind with a flood again. A less drastic way, Enki suggested, would be to let lions or disease control human numbers. Enlil agreed and even gave Utnapishtim and his wife immortality.

This story may sound familiar because it is basically the same as the Noah's Ark story in the Bible (Genesis, chapters 6 to 9). To the Mesopotamians, too, this was both myth and history. They recorded events as occurring so many years before and after "the Flood." Archaeologists have found evidence of massive flooding that destroyed large areas of Mesopotamia several times. In his excavations of Ur, Sir Leonard Woolley discovered traces of a flood that he calculated had been twenty-five feet deep and covered an area of thirty thousand square miles. The particular

This fourteenth-century painting of the biblical tale of Noah's flood is similar to the images in the more ancient story of Utnapishtim's flood. In the Mesopotamian story, a raven instead of a dove finds dry land.

flood probably referred to in the Sumerian tale occurred around 2800 B.C.E.

The Netherworld

Utnapishtim and his wife received immortality but were the only mortals to do so. The epic hero Gilgamesh sought the secret of immortality after the death of his great friend Enkidu, but Utnapishtim himself discouraged his quest, saying that permanence was not meant for humankind.

"Do we build a house forever? Does the river ever rise up and bring on floods? The dragonfly leaves its husk that its face might but glance at the face of the sun. Since the days of yore there has been no permanence. The restings of the dead, how alike they are!"

Similar advice was given Gilgamesh by the nymph Siduri. "When the gods created man, they allotted to him death, but life they retained in their own keeping. As for you, Gilgamesh, fill your belly with good things; day and night, night and day, feast and be merry, dance and rejoice. Let your clothes be fresh, bathe yourself in water, cherish the little child that holds your hand, make your wife happy in your embrace; for this too is the lot of man."

Indeed, the afterlife was nothing to look forward to. It was "the house which none leave who enter it, on the road from which there is no way back. . . where dust is their fare and clay their food, they are clothed like birds with wings for garments, and see no light, residing in darkness."

One myth tells how Ishtar, the goddess of love, descended through the seven gates to the Underworld hoping to win control of it from her older sister. The Queen of the Dead tricked her into having to stay, but Enki played his own trick and freed Ishtar. However, her lover, Tammuz, the fertility god, was sent to the Underworld in exchange, though it was agreed he could return to life for part of the year so that crops and animals could continue to grow.

This myth is similar to many Near Eastern and Mediterranean tales about dying and resurrected deities, including ancient Egypt's story of Isis and Osiris, and Greece's tale of Demeter and Persephone. The myths of the region may have influenced one another, but all were meant to explain one of humankind's earliest concerns: seasonal changes and the apparent decline and return of life.

To Mesopotamians, all things were in the hands of gods or demons. Here, Babylon's king Melishipak II (twelfth century B.C.E.) presents his ailing daughter to Nanai, goddess of health and medicine.

Haunted Mesopotamia

Perhaps because the Netherworld was particularly uninviting, the Mesopotamians worried a lot about returning ghosts as well as

CHARM AGAINST NIGHTMARES

The Mesopotamian deities were generally thought too busy to bother with the everyday lives of people. But they had a strong sense of justice, and if asked by some mortal in need, they might help. A person troubled by demons at night could wear an amulet with this incantation on it:

"The one which has approached the house scares me from my bed, rends me and makes me see nightmares. May they consign him to the god Bine, gatekeeper of the Underworld, by the decree of Ninurta, prince of the Underworld, by the decree of Marduk who dwells in Esagila in Babylon. Let door and bolt know that I am under the protection of the two lords."

With two major gods on his or her side, the Mesopotamian felt assured of finally getting a good night's sleep.

This bronze figure of the demon Pazuzu is inscribed, "I am Pazuzu, king of evil spirits and of the winds which come raging down from the mountains." Pazuzu also had a good side. He was so powerful he could protect believers from other evil spirits.

about various demons and evil magic workers.

If someone did not receive the proper burial rites or enough offerings after death, his or her ghost might wander and haunt the living. One of the worst things someone could do to an enemy was to leave the corpse unburied or tear it out of its tomb. This was sometimes deliberately done during war, presumably by soldiers who would then get far enough away to avoid any haunting.

If ghosts became particularly troublesome, special priests were called in to exorcise them with incantations and offerings. Sometimes the priest made a clay figure of the ghost and either gave it a proper burial or deformed it so that it could no longer cause harm. If a person was being haunted, a wax figure might be made of him or her and buried so that the ghosts would go away, thinking their victim had died.

Ghosts weren't Mesopotamians' only supernatural fear. Their world was filled with demons whose sole job was to cause trouble. Lamashtu killed babies and new mothers; Nergal caused plague; Pazuzu brought sandstorms from the desert; and Rabisu, the Croucher, lurked in doorways and dark corners. Many other demons abounded, some just nameless doers of evil.

A particularly troublesome demon might have to be driven

out by priests and ceremonies. But since demons were so common, many people wore amulets, magic charms to ward them off. These portrayed particular demons with inscriptions to make them powerless. Sometimes one demon was thought to protect against others.

There were good spirits, too, who might help people, and it was possible to create guardians to fight off evil spirits. Following exact rules, statuettes were made of clay or wood and placed at doorways and around or under the house. Some figures looked like people, while others were monstrous combinations of animals. Figures made to resemble fierce guard dogs had names like "Don't Stop to Think, Bite!" and "Catcher of the Enemy." Kings worried about demons, too, and Assyrian and Babylonian palaces were guarded by monumental creatures such as winged bulls and human-headed lions.

Another Mesopotamian fear was of witchcraft—mortal enemies calling down evil by spitting, by making and mistreating figures of their victims, or by casting various spells. The law took witchcraft seriously and gave the death penalty to witches, but it was priests and doctors who were called on to cure the effects of supposed witchcraft.

Finally, people could bring illness and misfortune on themselves by breaking various rules for living. These sins might offend a person's guardian spirit, driving it away and leaving the person open to evils. Some of the rules may seem petty today. On the first day of the month of Tashrit, for example, a person "shall not eat garlic or a scorpion will sting him." Other rules dealt with more important misbehavior, such as not respecting one's parents, lying, cheating in business, or killing one's neighbor.

The consequences of breaking these commandments were not punishment after death but illness and misfortune in life. Similarly, reward for good behavior was not a good existence in the hereafter, but long life, health, and prosperity here on earth. The idea that one's life would be judged after death, as found in ancient Egypt and in Christian beliefs, was foreign to the Mesopotamians. For them, life between the two rivers was its own reward and punishment.

CHAPTER FOUR

LIFE DECREED BY THE GODS

Ancient Mesopotamians believed that humans were created to be servants to the gods and that it was the gods who decreed people's fates. It's not surprising, then, that Mesopotamians put a lot of effort into doing what the gods wanted of them, into learning the fates decreed for them, and into trying to influence divine decisions in their favor.

Abodes of the Gods

Archaeology at pre-Sumerian sites shows that the first buildings in Mesopotamia that were not homes or storehouses were probably temples. At first these were simple rectangular structures of mud brick, each with an altar and a wall niche for a statue of a goddess or god. When a temple was rebuilt, a slightly larger and grander structure would be constructed on the ruins of the old. Gradually this appearance of temples on platforms became deliberate. Smaller platforms were built on larger ones until a many-storied pyramid was created, with a sanctuary on top. Such a structure was called a ziggurat.

The ziggurat was the distinctive style of Mesopotamian temples from Sumerian through Babylonian and Assyrian times. Though ziggurats looked somewhat like the Egyptian pyramids, they were in fact quite different. Pyramids were dark royal tombs. Ziggurats, bathed in light and air, were temples where gods and goddesses could descend to earth and where humans (at least their priests and priestesses) could climb partway to heaven.

Around the ziggurats were large temple complexes where thousands of people lived and worked. In Sumerian times much of the city's governmental and commercial activities took place in these sprawling temples. In later Babylonia and Assyria, palaces were often larger and grander than

A ziggurat rises platform by platform in a modern artist's view of the ancient city of Babylon.

temples, a reflection of the king's increased importance. Still, temple complexes and their ziggurats continued to be prominent features of Mesopotamian cities.

Figures of Constant Prayer

Ancient Mesopotamians were very concerned that their gods know how devotedly they worshiped and how worthy they were of divine favor. They prayed that the deities show their favor by giving them long and prosperous lives. But few ordinary people were allowed inside temples and nobody could spend all night and day praying in the temples. Those who could afford to do so had statues made, usually of stone, to act as prayerful stand-ins.

This statue has the hopeful smile, the large eyes, and the clasped hands of the substitute worshiper in Sumerian times.

In some pre-Sumerian sites these statues were simply stylized rectangles topped with large eyes. In Sumerian times they became more realistic, but the eyes were still emphasized, perhaps showing that the substitute worshiper was in constant, wakeful attention. The statues' hands were clasped, their faces hopeful, and sometimes they were inscribed with the worshiper's name and prayer. When statues became outdated, they were put under the temple floor.

Royal Agents of the Gods

Kings also placed statues of themselves in temples, but kings had a special relationship with the gods. Kingship was believed to have been "lowered from heaven" by Enlil, king of the gods. This was done twice, once before and once after the Flood. The king was to serve as the god's agent on earth and as his people's spokesman to the gods.

One of the chief ways the kings fulfilled these duties was to build and repair temples. Many royal inscriptions record these pious actions. Statues and reliefs show kings carrying bricks and baskets of mortar. Such figures were often placed under the foundations of temples to be permanent reminders of the king's devotion. A stone statue of Gudea of Lagash shows the ruler holding a temple plan in his lap, a plan that the gods supposedly showed him in a dream. Even those Assyrian kings who reveled in destroying cities left long inscriptions recording their building and repairing of temples.

The king had many other responsibilities, too. For one thing, he was supposed to hunt. Originally leaders might be expected to protect their people by killing wild animals. In time hunting became a ritualized way to show the king's role as protector. Lion hunting was a regular royal

King Gudea of Lagash fulfilled his duties to gods and men by building temples. This prayerful statue was placed in a new temple around 2100 B.C.E. to remind the gods of the king's devotion. On his lap is a temple floor plan.

activity, and for this purpose wild lions were rounded up by the hundreds. Later Mesopotamian kings had their own game parks, partly stocked with animals brought as foreign trade or tribute.

Other duties of the king as agent of the gods included building canals and defensive walls, and insuring justice. One of the insignia of kingship that the gods gave kings was "the scepter of justice." As Hammurabi proclaimed when setting down his law code, "When Marduk commissioned me to set right the people of the land and to cause them to have government, I set truth and justice throughout the land and made the people prosperous." Administering justice wasn't just a civil duty for the king, it was a religious one.

In early Sumerian times the king himself was not considered a god, but some later Mesopotamian kings used divine titles. Certainly the gods, through their priests and priestesses, were involved in choosing the next king from the many possible royal heirs.

Celebrations of the Divine

Throughout the year the king, the clergy, and sometimes the people were involved in ceremonies to please the gods and win their continued favor. The most sacred object in any temple was the statue of its special god or goddess. There, with the right ceremonies, the deity might actually dwell and make contact with humans. The figures were usually made of precious woods covered with gold and jewels. Daily ceremonies by priests and priestesses kept the statues bathed, clothed, and fed.

Worshipers placed statues like this one in the temples, believing that these figures prayed for their owners' souls.

Eating was definitely a divine activity. After all, one reason the gods created humankind in the first place was to take over the tedious tasks of growing and preparing food. Several times a day, large amounts of food and drink were served to the temple deities, behind curtains. The "leftovers" were distributed to royalty or the temple staff. Deities also seemed to take pleasure and nourishment from smelling burning incense.

ANIMAL OMENS

Here are a few of the hundreds of actions by animals that could predict human fate.

- ❖ If black ants are seen in the foundations that have been laid, that house will get built, and the owner will live to grow old.

- ❖ If red ants are seen, the owner of that house will die before his time.

- ❖ If a snake passes from right to left of a man, he will have a good name.

- ❖ If a snake passes from left to right of a man, he will have a bad name.

- ❖ If a snake appears in a place where a man and wife are standing and talking, the man and wife will divorce.

- ❖ If a scorpion lurks in a man's bed, that man will have riches.

- ❖ If ants kill one another, making a battle. . . there will be the downfall of a great army.

- ❖ If an ox has tears in both of its eyes, some evil will befall the owner.

- ❖ If a fox runs into the public square, that town will be devastated.

- ❖ If a white dog urinates on a man, hard times will seize the man.

- ❖ If a red dog urinates on a man, that man will have happiness.

Once a person understood what an omen meant, there were often ways to avert evil predictions. For example, if you had been the victim of a urinating white dog, "You shall make a dog of clay. You shall put cedar wood on its neck. You shall pour oil on its head. You shall clothe it in a goatskin. You shall pull hairs from a horse's mane as the tail."

You would then take the clay dog model to a riverbank and set up an altar with offerings of bread, dates, honey, butter, and beer. For a fee, a priest would recite incantations and get the gods to remove the evil.

In the future, then, you would stay away from ill-behaved white dogs.

Common people as well as priests made offerings of food and incense to the gods during special festivals.

Particularly important festivals were ones in which the divine statues were paraded in public and taken to visit other gods or to sacred sites outside the city. These statues might also be subject to less pleasant travel if they were carried off from their hometowns by conquering enemies. A town that had lost the figure of its patron deity was in big trouble until the statue was returned.

By Babylonian times several important festivals had been merged into a grand, eleven-day New Year's celebration. This took place near the spring equinox (around March 21). It was the time when the gods set destinies for the coming year, and people hoped that by ritually reenacting their mythical history and reminding the gods of their devotion, these destinies might be good ones.

Special ceremonies were performed on each day of the festival. The creation tale was recited or performed on the fourth day. On the fifth day a sheep was beheaded. After being magically made to absorb the old year's evil, the sheep was thrown into the river so that the evil would be carried away.

Also on the fifth day the king was ceremonially humiliated to remind him that he was merely a mortal servant of the gods. His royal regalia were taken from him and a priest pulled his ears and slapped his face until his eyes teared.

Later in the festival the king, fully royal again, escorted a statue of the god Marduk (who in Babylon had taken on Enlil's role) to a special shrine outside the city. The Sumerian fertility festival of the Sacred Marriage was also made part of the Babylonian New Year's festival. In this ceremony the king and a priestess entered into a symbolic marriage to assure good crops for the following year.

Burying the Dead

Since prehistoric times Mesopotamians buried their dead with grave goods such as pottery, weapons, jewelry, and special possessions. In other cultures, such as ancient Egypt's, this practice seems to have been linked to the idea that these things might be useful to the dead person in the afterlife. But if the gloomy view of the Netherworld in Mesopotamian writings was popularly believed, it's not clear how much use such goods would be there.

Possibly fine things were placed in graves to properly honor the dead person and persuade his or her ghost not to haunt the living. Or grave goods might have made some small difference in the quality of a person's afterlife. Either the spirit could use them directly to relieve its boredom, or perhaps they could be offered to the deities of the Netherworld so that the spirit would get slightly better treatment.

Most Mesopotamians were buried in coffins or lying on their sides, wrapped in mats. Prominent family members and children were some-

The ruins of a ziggurat overlook the "great death pit" of Ur, where the bodies of seventy-four people were found in what archaeologists believe was a mass sacrificial burial.

times buried under the floor of the house or in back near the family shrine, while others were buried in cemeteries outside of town. A grave might be opened several times to add new people. Unfortunately time, salty soil, and grave robbers have destroyed much of what might be learned from Mesopotamian graves, particularly those of common people.

But one group of graves from the Sumerian period has revealed some startling customs. Whether all of these graves were royal or not, they were certainly for people of importance. In these burials the primary occupant was accompanied not only by lavish grave goods but by a number of human attendants, who apparently went alive to their graves.

Outside one tomb, in what excavator Leonard Woolley called the "great death pit," seventy-four human bodies were found, along with carts and oxen. Many beautiful objects there escaped looters because the deep pit was filled solidly with dirt and other offerings.

Cups found beside the bodies suggest that the women, musicians, soldiers, and animal tenders were drugged or poisoned. The excavator found no signs of struggle. Even the delicate headdresses of the women were properly in place. One girl appeared to have been slow getting ready; instead of putting her silver ribbon in her hair like her companions, she wadded it up in her pocket.

Knowing as little as we do about their beliefs, it is hard today to understand how these people were willing to accompany their masters or mistresses into death. Similar mass sacrificial burials are known from other parts of the world, but this is the only certain example from Mesopotamia.

Seeking the Will of the Gods

Since Mesopotamians saw their fates as being totally in the hands of the gods, it is understandable that they went to great lengths to find out what those fates were. Among the most important class of priesthood were the Baru, the diviners. These men and women studied various signs for clues about the future.

Diviners had specialties just as medical doctors do today. Some looked at the livers or entrails of sacrificial animals for answers to questions. These diviners even had precise clay models of livers to consult for the meaning of different marks. Other diviners studied the way oil spread on water. Watching the behavior of animals or the flight of birds was

This clay model of a sheep's liver is inscribed to tell diviners the meaning of marks in various places.

another specialty. Observing natural events, the weather, or the movements of stars and planets also gave clues to the future.

Dreams could foretell the future as well. Specialized diviners interpreted the meaning of dreams, and sometimes people deliberately asked the gods for dreams that would give them the answer to some problem. In the *Epic of Gilgamesh,* the main characters repeatedly learn of the future, both good and bad, from dreams.

Diviners were a vital part of Mesopotamian life. Kings consulted them before taking most actions, and diviners always accompanied the armies, sometimes serving as generals. Private individuals could report an omen or significant dream to a diviner, but they also had to give a lock of their hair and fringe from their clothes so that the priest or priestess could magically determine if

IF YOU LIVED IN MESOPOTAMIA

If you had been born in Babylon during the reign of Hammurabi, around 1780 B.C.E., your way of life would have been determined by the facts of your birth—whether you were a boy or a girl, rich or poor, slave or free. With this chart you can trace the course your life might have taken if you were a member of a middle-class family.

You were born in Babylon. . . .

As a Boy . . .   **As a Girl . . .**

You and your brothers and sisters live in a one-story, windowless house of mud brick. Your father, a scribe in the temple of Marduk, is often away, so you are raised by your mother, your grandmother, and the household slaves. Your mother makes you wear an amulet around your neck to protect you from demons. You most enjoy playing with your dog and your clay toys and hearing the storytellers at the market.

At age six you start scribe school, going every day from sunrise to sunset but getting New Year's and other festival times off. Your teacher is very strict, sometimes caning you for talking in class or not finishing your assignments. Still, you enjoy making the crisp cuneiform marks on wet clay and learning about the doings of kings a thousand years ago.

At age six your mother, grandmother, and family slaves begin to teach you how to cook, spin, and manage a household. Sometimes your brother shows you how to write cuneiform signs. You wish you could go to scribe school, too, but at least you have more time than he does to go to hear the storytellers at the market.

As a young man you have finished scribe school, and your family has arranged for you to marry the daughter of a wealthy wool merchant. You've decided to work for your father-in-law rather than for the temple because a job keeping business records may mean you will have the chance to travel on caravans to distant places like Ur and Ebla.

As a young woman you are about to marry the son of a general your father met at court. Your family has arranged the marriage. You are busy making your wedding clothes and learning about makeup, and often you go to the temple of Ishtar to pray that you will have lots of sons so that your husband won't want to marry a second wife.

As a man you have learned many languages on trading trips, so sometimes you are sent on diplomatic missions for the king. You are now wealthy enough to have a two-story house with inlaid wooden furniture. To insure continued prosperity, you make regular offerings to the gods and take your wife and children to all of the public ceremonies at the temples.

As a woman you live in a fine two-story house and enjoy the jewelry and treasures your husband brings back from war. You get along fairly well with your husband's second wife. Since you have sons and she does not, you can run the household, and your children—not hers—will inherit.

When you die, your family will bury you and some of your finest things under the pavement behind the house. They will make regular offerings to your spirit at the family chapel so that your ghost will not come back and bother them.

58

their message was a true one. Extensive records were kept of divinations, and these were consulted when similar predictions were needed.

Mesopotamians were fatalistic, but often they didn't just accept whatever fate had in store for them. Most predictions depended on the occurrence of a certain series of events. Once a person learned of some bad fate in store, she or he could sometimes change the actions that would have led to it or perform certain rituals that would cancel the predicted ill fate. Diviners could tell which days were favorable or unfavorable for certain activities. People could then plan their actions accordingly—whether they were launching an invasion or selling a goat.

Astrologers and other diviners were particularly concerned about the fates of kings. If omens predicted the king's death or misfortune, a substitute king might be crowned, be allowed to "rule" for a time, and then be killed and buried with all the royal honors. Assyria's Esarhaddon, a particularly fretful king, had at least six substitutes crowned during his reign between 680 and 669 B.C.E. But such attempts to trick fate didn't always work. Around 1860 B.C.E. Erra-imitt, the king of Isin, sought to avert his predicted death by installing a gardener as substitute king. Afterward, however, Erra-imitt died while drinking hot soup in his palace, and the gardener ruled Isin for the next twenty-four years.

It may seem to us that Mesopotamians were gloomy people, feeling that life was so totally out of their control. But at least they didn't have the stress of feeling responsible for everything that happens in life. And by learning the rules and working within them, Mesopotamians felt they could win the chance for a good, long life.

CHAPTER FIVE

PERSISTENCE OF THE PAST

To say that Mesopotamia was the cradle of civilization does not mean simply that the people living between the Tigris and Euphrates won some sort of historical race by being the first to become civilized. Mesopotamia did more than just "get there first." It influenced many of its neighbors, helping to spark their own rise to civilization.

Art from ancient Egypt and India shows these areas had contact with Mesopotamia at a time when they were just developing their own civilizations. Although the cultures and the writing systems of each developed differently, the example of Mesopotamia was clearly important.

During the thousands of years that Mesopotamia was a power in the Near East, its art, religion, and political system influenced many people in the area. When Mesopotamia was conquered by Persia and later by Greece and then Rome, much of its learning and way of life passed into those civilizations and, through them, into Europe and the modern Western world.

Traces are clear even in modern North American society. Some of these are in grand things such as living under the rule or law, or in our religious beliefs. But even in everyday life Mesopotamia's legacy is with us. A morning's glance at the clock, the calendar, or newspaper horoscope, or even a ride to school in a wheeled vehicle—all are ties we have to those curious, inventive, and complex people who lived long ago between the two rivers.

Much in the "land between the rivers" has changed and much is the same. This modern Iraqi boy selling ducks in front of an Islamic mosque may be descended from children who sold their farm produce in front of Mesopotamian ziggurats.

Legacy of Literacy

Mesopotamians were not only the first people to write; they were the first who had a literature. Their writings influenced many neighboring peoples, and the echoes of their stories can still be heard today.

The Old Testament patriarch Abraham "became a great nation" after leading his people, the Hebrews, from the land of Ur. The Mesopotamian influences that the "Habiru" brought with them were strengthened by centuries of trade contact and then by the years of captivity in Babylon after Nebuchadrezzar destroyed Jerusalem.

The Old Testament version of the flood is basically a retelling of the

REMEMBERING SENNACHERIB

"The Assyrian came down like the wolf on the fold,
His cohorts were gleaming in purple and gold;
And the sheen of their spears was like stars on the sea,
When the blue wave rolls nightly on deep Galilee."

With this the nineteenth-century English poet Lord Byron begins his poem "The Destruction of Sennacherib." He based his version on the biblical account in Kings, chapters 18 and 19. There Sennacherib, king of Assyria, says to Hezekiah, king of Judah, "Behold, you have heard what the kings of Assyria have done to all the lands, destroying them utterly. And shall you be delivered? Have the gods of the nations delivered them, the nations which my fathers destroyed. . . ?

But Hezekiah prays to his God, "and that night the angel of the Lord went forth and slew a hundred and eighty five thousand in the camp of the Assyrians. . . . Then Sennacherib, King of Assyria, departed and went home and dwelt at Nineveh."

Or as Byron puts it:

"For the Angel of Death spread his wings on the blast,
And breathed in the face of the foe as he passed;

. . . .

And the tents were all silent, the banners alone,
The lances unlifted, the trumpets unblown."

This was not quite the way Sennacherib himself recorded it. In his annals the Assyrian makes no mention of any plague that hit his camp and ended his siege of Jerusalem. Instead he claims that he left because he got what he wanted. He lists all the gold, jewels, ivory, furniture, and women he won in tribute; and "as for Hezekiah, the terrifying splendor of my majesty overcame him."

Which goes to show that not all ancient records are always recording pure "history." Here one writer wrote history to glorify his God, and another wrote it to glorify himself—leaving the modern historian, and the poet, pretty much on their own.

earlier Mesopotamian story, with the many gods changed to the one Hebrew God. Other similarities between Mesopotamian and biblical stories are seen in the wording and ideas of many parts of Proverbs and Psalms. The Book of Job is a longer, more poetic version of a Sumerian story in which a righteous and prosperous man suffers many disasters. He complains to his god but accepts his fate. In the end he is rewarded for his steadfast faith and is restored to happiness.

More parallels between the Bible and Mesopotamian mythology may now go unnoticed because the Mesopotamian originals are lost. But by being preserved in the Hebrew scriptures, Mesopotamian stories and ways of thought have come down to us and influenced many aspects of Western culture.

Another important piece of Mesopotamian literature is the *Epic of Gilgamesh*. It was not only written on clay tablets, but was also one of the tales told by professional storytellers in public markets and at festivals. For thousands of years it was popular throughout the Near East. It may have been an inspiration for later adventure tales such as the Greek stories about Hercules and Odysseus.

But the *Epic of Gilgamesh* is more than just a literary influence— it's a mighty good story. Gilgamesh, a strong but arrogant king of Uruk, is put in check when the gods create Enkidu, a wild man of equal strength, whom they then have tamed and brought to Uruk. There he fights and then befriends Gilgamesh, and the two heroes set off on fantastic adventures, seeing wonders and fighting monsters. In the process they make enemies of some important deities, and Enkidu dies. Gilgamesh, torn by grief and now fearful of death himself, sets out to seek eternal life. Although after more adventures he fails in this quest, he comes to accept the life the gods made for him.

The story is exciting and contains some beautiful writing, but it also shows that five thousand years ago people thought about many of the same things we think about today.

Enduring Art

Art historians can trace the influence of Mesopotamian art into ancient Egypt, India, Persia, and throughout the Near East. When the Greeks and Romans conquered Mesopotamia, they absorbed some of the local art

The Epic of Gilgamesh *not only entertained Mesopotamians for thousands of years, it was a frequent subject for Mesopotamian artists. Here a carving from the palace of King Sargon II of Assyria shows Gilgamesh taming a lion.*

and passed these influences into Europe. Today traces can still be seen in Western art and architecture. The fluted column, based on Mesopotamian bundled reed columns, is just one example.

After Mesopotamia was rediscovered by nineteenth-century archaeologists, interest in this ancient culture started a new wave of Mesopotamian influence in art. Mesopotamian designs and themes appeared in Victorian architecture, paintings, poetry, and even jewelry. This continued into the twentieth century, and some of the grand movie theaters of the 1920s looked as if they themselves could be sets for biblical epic films.

Much of the way Mesopotamia was shown in later art came from its presentation in the Bible, and since Babylon and Assyria were the Hebrews' enemies, this is a largely negative picture. In many paintings, movies, and novels, the Tower of Babel and the Babylonian royal court are shown as being the height of sin and decadence.

The idea of Babylon as a city of sin has come down to us from the Bible. This elaborate scene is from the movie Intolerance, *which was made in the early part of the twentieth century.*

Not all of the surviving images of Mesopotamia are negative, though—as anyone who's ever played with a Noah's ark set knows!

Technology from the Two Rivers

It is not surprising that, as the world's first civilization, Mesopotamia was the birthplace of many of the skills we associate with civilization. Not only farming, but also pottery, metalworking, and cloth making first appeared in the Mesopotamian region. Making pottery on a wheel instead of by hand probably began there well before 4000 B.C.E.

The pottery wheel may also have inspired another important invention, the wheel for transportation. Around 3500 B.C.E., Sumerians mounted their sledges onto wheels, making it possible for animals to pull many times their weight and for the Mesopotamian battle chariot to become a major engine of war. These early wheels were made of solid wood and were often rimmed with metal studs. Later the Hittites and then the Egyptians refined the idea with spoked wheels on lighter two-wheel chariots.

It is probable, of course, that if the Mesopotamians hadn't invented the wheel, someone else would have. But some advanced civilizations, such as those of Central and South America, never did use the wheel. It is fair, therefore, to trace every wheeled vehicle today—whether the tractor, the skateboard, or the family car—back to some ancient Mesopotamian inventor.

Another first for Mesopotamia, which some civilizations never hit on independently, was the arch. This is an architectural technique by which wedge-shaped bricks or stones fit together in a semicircular shape. An arch can span much more space and carry much more weight than can a flat beam or roof. Since the upper portions of most Mesopotamian buildings are long gone, it's hard to tell how much use they made of the arch, but it is known from tombs and gateways. Later the Romans made the arch a major part of their architecture, and its use spread around the world.

Science in the Gods' Hands

The ancient Mesopotamians didn't draw the line that we do today between science and magic. To them, both were part of explaining the world and the order the gods gave to it. Yet many of the true sciences that we now recognize began in Mesopotamia.

Mathematics, necessary for commerce and architecture, developed in Mesopotamia to a high degree. The Mesopotamian number system was based on 60 and on numbers that divide evenly into 60, such as 12. It survives today in our 360-degree circle, 12-hour clock, and 60-minute hour. Ancient cuneiform tablets give multiplication tables and algebra formulas. There were even school texts with word problems about the geometry needed for building canals or defense walls.

The Mesopotamians were also the first people to establish a system of weights and measures. Standardized measurements were needed to provide for a fair exchange of goods and to be sure that building plans would work. The standards were not always the same from city to city or from time period to time period, but they allowed people who worked together to agree on what they were doing.

Measurement of weight was based on real things such as "a donkey load" or "a man load." These were then represented in

Mesopotamians were the first people to use the arch in architecture. Wedges set into a semicircle make it possible for doorways and roofs to span more space and hold more weight. This arch in the ruins of Babylon survived for thousands of years.

standardized weights made of metal or stone in the shape of lions or ducks. Distances were measured in a similar way, with "a finger," "a foot," "a reed," and "a pole" representing standard lengths that could then be used to measure other things. Liquids were measured in pots of fixed sizes—not unlike our "cup" measurements today.

Mesopotamian astronomers were quite advanced. They could accurately predict eclipses of the sun and moon and could

The invention of wheeled vehicles around 3500 B.C.E. was one of Mesopotamia's greatest contributions to human technology. This clay model of a chariot was made nearly four thousand years ago.

plot the positions of the stars and planets and the phases of the moon. They didn't do this for pure knowledge but so that they could plan and predict earthly events. Today they would be considered astrologers as much as astronomers.

These Mesopotamians named the twelve constellations of the zodiac and thought that earthly happenings could be predicted by the positions of the moon and planets among the stars. They also believed that a person's fate could be determined by the patterns in the sky when she or he was born. This idea became popular in the ancient world and is still with us today in horoscopes.

Another use for astronomy in Mesopotamia was to establish a standard year, something important in deciding when to plant and harvest crops. Like many people, the Mesopotamians based their months on the 28 days it takes the moon to go through its phases. However, units of 28 days did not fit neatly into the 365 days it takes the sun to mark a year, so extra short months were thrown into the calendar to make everything come out evenly. As with other measurements, however, these systems varied from place to place and time to time, so often modern historians have trouble deciding exactly when things happened even when the ancient Mesopotamians gave dates.

A Land of Laws

Early Mesopotamians discovered both the advantages and the disadvantages of civilization. When a number of individuals live close together and join in commercial and social activities, they are bound to have disputes. Rules are needed to settle disputes. Civilization requires law.

Probably most of the early Mesopotamian states had their own laws, and fragments of some of these have been found. Among the oldest discovered so far is the law code of Ur-Nammu from around 2050 B.C.E.

To begin it, the king points out that in doing his job for the gods and bringing order and safety to the city, he must first "establish justice in the land." He must insure that "the orphan was not given over to the rich man, the widow was not given over to the powerful man, the man of one shekel [measure of small worth] was not given over to the man of one mina [measure of larger worth]."

Ur-Nammu's and other early codes deal with matters such as mar-

A FEW OF HAMMURABI'S LAWS

❖ If a man has accused someone and has cast an accusation of murder against him and has not proved it, the accuser shall be put to death.

❖ If a man has committed robbery and is arrested, that man shall be put to death. If the robber is not arrested, the robbed man shall certify before the god what of his that is lost, and the city or the mayor within whose territory the robbery was committed shall replace the lost thing for him.

❖ If a son has struck his father, they shall cut off his hand.

❖ If a man has opened his ditch for irrigation and has been slack and consequently has caused the water to carry away his neighbor's field, he shall pay corn corresponding [to the crop lost].

❖ If a man is in the grip of debt and has handed over his wife, son or daughter for silver, or has given [them] into bondservice, for three years they shall serve in the house of their buyer or the one who took them into bondservice; in the fourth year their release shall be granted.

❖ If a man's bride has borne him sons and his slave-girl has borne him sons, and the father in his lifetime says to the sons whom the slave-girl has borne him, "You are my sons," he shall count them with the sons of the bride. After the father has gone to his fate, the sons of the bride and the sons of the slave-girl shall share equally in the property of the father's estate. The heir, a son of the bride, shall take [first] choice at the division.

❖ If a surgeon has made a deep incision in a freeman with a bronze instrument and saved the man's life. . . he shall take ten shekels of silver. If a surgeon has made a deep incision in a freeman with a bronze instrument and caused the man to die. . . they shall cut off his hand.

❖ If a man has cast a charge of [using] black magic against a man and has not proved it, the man charged with black magic shall go to the Holy River and jump into the Holy River. If the Holy River clutches him, his accuser shall take his estate. If the Holy River clears the man and he comes safely back, he who cast the charge of black magic against him shall be put to death. He who jumped into the Holy River shall take his accuser's estate.

riage and divorce, false accusation, theft, runaway and insolent slaves, debt, inheritance, land rights, and personal injury. When it came to penalties, these laws established a principle that a fixed fine would be paid to an injured party depending on the severity of the crime. The law code of

Eshunna gives the fine for biting off a person's nose or for putting out an eye as one mina, while for knocking out a tooth it is only half a mina.

The law code of Hammurabi, king of Babylon from 1792 to 1750 B.C.E., is the most famous today because it has survived on clay tablets and also was carved into a large slab of black stone. Under a relief carving of Hammurabi receiving his laws from a god, the king is quoted as saying that his purpose in writing the code was "to cause justice to prevail in the land, to destroy the wicked and evil, that the strong may not oppress the weak."

By Hammurabi's time, more purely Semitic thinking had replaced some earlier Sumerian ideas. Often, instead of paying a fine, the wrongdoer had to suffer the same fate she or he had inflicted on others. "If a man puts out the eye of a man, they shall put out his eye." However, Mesopotamian justice, like its society, was divided by class. If the man whose eye was put out was not a free landowner, the wrongdoer kept his eyes and paid a fine of one mina instead.

This justice was very exact. "If a builder has constructed a house. . . with the result that the house he built collapses and so caused the death of the owner, the builder shall be put to death. If it has caused the death of the son of the owner of the house, they shall put to death the son of the builder."

This Semitic "eye for an eye, tooth for a tooth" principle of law was also used by the early Hebrews and passed into Western culture from there. Today it has been largely replaced by the wrongdoer having to pay fines or spend time in jail, but the death penalty for murder is a modern remnant of retributive law.

In all, 282 laws were recorded in Hammurabi's code. Their significance today is not so much in the survival of individual laws or legal principles but in the idea that a complex society must be governed by law. That principle, basic to our modern world, was learned long ago—at the dawn of civilization.

Preserving a Legacy

Mesopotamia was indeed the cradle of civilization, and its archaeological remains still promise new discoveries. But the land between the rivers is not simply a place of ancient ruins and past achievements. History continues there in the modern nation of Iraq.

Political upheaval, which marked ancient Mesopotamian history, continues in modern Iraq. These refugees from recent warfare face an uncertain future, as many people in that area have for thousands of years.

After the final collapse of Babylon, Mesopotamia's long history was filled with change and foreign domination. Today it is an independent Islamic nation, but under the surface much of the older way of life remains. And throughout the centuries Mesopotamia has remained active in world history, often in ways that have grown directly from its past.

Ancient Mesopotamians struggled to live with people from the northern hills, fought with countries on their east, and contended with other powerful nations. Today Iraq struggles with the Kurds of the northern hills, fights with Iran to the east, and contends with other world powers.

Although Mesopotamia may once have been the Garden of Eden, it has known little tranquility since. Today the power of modern weaponry can destroy not only living people, but also evidence of the past. Iraqi archaeologists and their colleagues from around the world have worked hard to preserve and study the region's past. But in recent warfare many monuments and archaeological sites have been damaged or destroyed, forever losing pieces of history. Assurbanipal's palace at Nineveh and Ur-Nammu's great ziggurat at Ur are among the many casualties.

It is not only the descendants of ancient Mesopotamians who suffer from this loss. The legacy of Mesopotamia is our common legacy. In many ways, Mesopotamia was the cradle of us all.

Mesopotamia: A Chronology

11,000	The dog becomes the first domestic animal
10,000	Farming begins in mountains north of Mesopotamia
8000	Pottery appears in the Near East
6500	Copper used in Mesopotamia
6000	Mixing of farming and nomadic cultures in Mesopotamia
4500	Invention of the plow
4300	Beginning of Mesopotamian cities in Sumer
3500	The first wheeled vehicles
3100	The beginning of writing
2900	Beginning of Sumerian domination of southern Mesopotamia; Kish supreme city in Sumer
2650	Gilgamesh is king of Uruk, dominant city in Sumer
2350	Sargon I controls Akkad and Sumer
2100	Ur-Nammu king of Ur, dominant city in Sumer
1900	Amorite dynasties control Mesopotamia
1810	Shamshi-Adad rules Assyria
1792	Hammurabi becomes king of Babylon
1595	Hittites sack Babylon
1500	Kassites control Babylon; Mitanni conquers Assyria
1350	Assyrian empire expands
1171	Elamites conquer Babylon
1100	Tiglath-Pileser I, king of Assyria, battles Arameans
883	Ashurnasirpal II becomes king of Assyria and expands empire
744	Tiglath-Pileser III of Assyria reorganizes the empire
704	Sennacherib, king of Assyria, begins reign; besieges Jerusalem, attacks Babylon
664	Assurbanipal II expands Assyrian Empire to Egypt
612	Assyria invaded by Medes and Babylonians
605	Babylon defeats Assyria and Egypt at Carchemish
597	Nebuchadrezzar II destroys Jerusalem
539	Cyrus of Persia captures Babylon

GLOSSARY

aristocracy: the upper class in a society

bitumen: naturally occurring asphalt used in ancient times as cement or waterproofing

civilization: a high level of culture and technology, usually associated with living in cities

deportation: the practice of removing large groups of people from their home territories and forcing them to settle somewhere else

divination: predicting the future from certain signs

dynasty: a series of rulers in the same family or the time period in which a series of related rulers governed an area

epic: a long poetic tale, usually with extraordinary heroes and adventures

exorcise: to drive out an evil demon or ghost

guild: an organized group of people in the same trade or craft; guilds looked out for the interests of its members

irrigation: a system for artificially putting water on agricultural fields

millennium: a period of one thousand years; plural is *millennia*

mosaic: a picture or design made by fitting together bits of stone, glass, or tile of different colors and then cementing them in place

nomads: people with no permanent homes who follow sources of wild food or accompany their herds

obsidian: naturally occurring volcanic glass, usually black

omen: an indication of some future happening

relief: a sculpture where the design projects from a flat surface

Semitic: a group of related languages spoken in the Near East and Africa; people who speak those languages. Modern Semitic languages include Arabic and Hebrew.

tribute: a payment of money or goods by a subject people to their foreign ruler

FOR FURTHER READING

Bauman, Hans. *The Land of Ur.* New York: Pantheon Books, 1969.

Foster, Leila Merrell. *Iraq.* Chicago: Children's Press, 1990.

Glubok, Shirley, ed. *Discovering the Royal Tombs at Ur.* New York: Macmillan, 1969.

Gray, John. *Near Eastern Mythology.* New York: Peter Bedrick Books, 1982.

Gregor, Arthur S. *How the World's First Cities Began.* New York: Dutton, 1967.

Hamblin, Dora Jane, and the editors of Time-Life Books. *The First Cities.* New York: Time-Life Books, 1973.

Hunter, Erica. *First Civilizations.* New York: Facts on File, 1994.

Kramer, Samuel Noah, and the editors of Time-Life Books. *Cradle of Civilization.* New York: Time-Life Books, 1967.

Lynch, James Michael. *Sumer, Cities of Eden.* Alexandria, Virginia: Time-Life Books, 1993.

Powers, Richard. *Land of the Two Rivers.* Cleveland: World Publishing Company, 1962.

Raintree Steck Vaughn. *Civilizations of the Middle East.* Austin, Texas: 1992.

Roaf, Michael. *Cultural Atlas of Mesopotamia and the Ancient Near East.* New York: Facts on File, 1990.

Robinson, Charles. *The First Book of Mesopotamia and Persia.* New York: Franklin Watts, 1962.

Severy, Merle. "Iraq, Crucible of Civilization," National Geographic, May 1991: 102–115.

Swisher, Clarice. *The Ancient Near East.* San Diego: Lucent Books, 1995.

Tubb, Jonathan N. *Bible Lands.* New York: Alfred Knopf, 1991.

Weisgard, L. *The Beginning of Cities.* New York: Coward-McCann, 1968.

BIBLIOGRAPHY

Bootero, Jean. "The First Law Code." In *Forty Centuries*. Britannica Society, 1972.

Byron, George (Lord). "The Destruction of Sennacherib." In *The Poetical Works of Byron*. Boston: Houghton Mifflin Co., 1973.

Crawford, Harriet. *Sumer and the Sumerians*. Cambridge: Cambridge University Press, 1991.

Dalley, Stephanie. *Myths from Mesopotamia*. Oxford: Oxford University Press, 1989.

Delaport, L. *Mesopotamia, the Babylonian and Assyrian Civilizations*. New York: Barnes and Noble, 1970.

Frankfort, Henri. *The Birth of Civilization in the Near East*. New York: Doubleday, 1956.

Luckenbill, Daniel David. *Ancient Records of Assyria and Babylon*. 2 vols. Chicago: University of Chicago Press, 1926–1927.

Mallowan, M. E. L. *Early Mesopotamia and Iran*. London: Thames and Hudson, 1965.

Moorey, P. R. S. *Ancient Mesopotamian Materials and Industries*. Oxford: Oxford University Press, Clarendon Press, 1994.

Moscati, Sabatino. *The Face of the Ancient Orient*. Garden City: Doubleday, 1962.

Oates, Joan. *Babylon*. London: Thames and Hudson, 1986.

Oppenheim, A. Leo. *Ancient Mesopotamia*. Chicago: University of Chicago Press, 1964.

Saggs, H. W. F. *The Greatness That Was Babylon*. London: Sidgwick and Jackson, 1988.

Saggs, H. W. F. *The Might That Was Assyria*. London: Sidgwick and Jackson, 1984.

Sanders, N. K. *The Epic of Gilgamesh*. London: Penguin Books, 1972.

Woolley, Sir Leonard. *Excavations at Ur*. New York: Thomas Y. Crowell, 1954.

INDEX

Page numbers for illustrations are in boldface

ABOUT THE AUTHOR

Pamela Service grew up in Berkeley, California, and received a degree in political science there from the University of California. She went on to earn a masters degree in African prehistory from the University of London. She now lives with her family in Bloomington, Indiana, where she worked for seventeen years as a museum curator, serves on the Bloomington city council, and writes for children.

Among her published works of fiction are fifteen books which often combine fantasy, science fiction, and history. She is the author of *The Ancient African Kingdom of Kush* in this series. It was while studying Kush and Egypt in London that she became interested in the other ancient cultures of the region including Mesopotamia.